Find Your Future in Mathematics

Kelly Gunzenhauser

Created and produced by
Bright Futures Press, Cary, North Carolina
www.brightfuturespress.com

Published by
Cherry Lake Publishing, Ann Arbor, Michigan
www.cherrylakepublishing.com

Photo Credits: cover, Shutterstock/Aleyzel; cover, Shutterstock/Mclek; cover, Shutterstock/Zadorazhnyi Viktor; cover, Shutterstock/empics; cover, Shutterstock/Khakimulllin Aleksandr; page 4 (top), Shutterstock/zimmytws; page 4 (left), Shutterstock/grmark; page 6, Shutterstock/Khakimullin Aleksandr; page 6, (left) Shutterstock/Nerthuz; page 7, Shutterstock/Iconic Bestiary; page 8, Shutterstock/Mr Cheangchai Noojuntuk; page 9 (top), Shutterstock/Aleksandr Mijatovic; page 9 (left), Shutterstock/inxti; page 10, Shutterstock/Falara; page 11, Shutterstock/Barna Tanko; page 12 (top), Shutterstock/empics; page 12 (left), Shutterstock/ISebyl; page 13, Shutterstock/Moloko88; page 14, Shutterstock/Everything; page 15 (top), Shutterstock/Mclek; page 15 (left), Shutterstock/PHILIP IMAGE; page 16, Shutterstock/AXpop; page 17, Shutterstock/Laborant; page 18 (top), Shutterstock Zadirizhnyi Viktor; page 18 (left), Shutterstock/travellight; page 19, Shutterstock/Lorelyn Medina; page 20, Shutterstock/Ti_ser; page 21 (top), Shutterstock/Brian P Gielcyzk; page 21 (left), Shutterstock/Chones; page 22, Shutterstock/Tomacco; page 23, Shutterstock/Alex Staroseltsev; page 24 (top), Shutterstock/Dmitry Kalinovsky; page 24 (left), Shutterstock/Everett Historical; page 25, Shutterstock/Masha Tace; page 26, Shutterstock/yuttana jeenammol; page 27 (top), Shutterstock/Aleyzel; page 27 (left) Shutterstock/Kichigin; page 28, Shutterstock/leospaiens; page 29, Shutterstock/IM_photo.

Library of Congress Cataloging-in-Publication Data

Names: Gunzenhauser, Kelly. author.
Title: Find your future in mathematics / By Kelly Gunzenhauser.
Description: Ann Arbor, Michigan : Cherry Lake Publishing, [2016] | Series:
    Find your future in STEAM | Audience: Grades 4 to 6. | Includes index.
Identifiers: LCCN 2016006588| ISBN 9781634719025 (hardcover) | ISBN
    9781634719483 (pbk.) | ISBN 9781634719254 (pdf) | ISBN 9781634719711
    (ebook)
Subjects: LCSH: Mathematics--Vocational guidance--Juvenile literature. |
    Mathematicians--Juvenile literature.
Classification: LCC QA10.5 .G86 2016 | DDC 510.23--dc23
LC record available at https://lccn.loc.gov/2016006588

Printed in the United States of America.

Table of Contents

Find Your Future in Mathematics

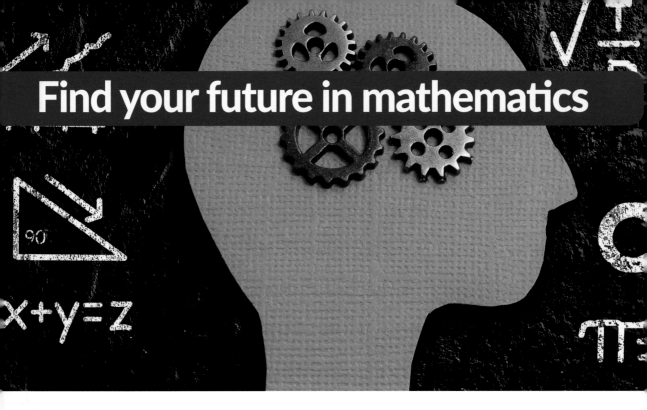

Find your future in mathematics

Every kid has probably said more than once, "Why do I have to learn all this math?" Believe it or not, math is useful, important, and it sneaks into some unexpected places. Everyone needs math skills to be more successful in life.

Want to know how your favorite athletic teams are doing? It takes math to find out. Need to plan how much allowance to save to buy that new video game? Math. Want to create a secret, unbreakable code? You guessed it. Math again!

Math is not only an important life skill, it also offers some very exciting ways to make a living. Many types of employers will pay you to use math to help them work faster, more accurately, and more efficiently.

This book and other titles in the *Find Your Future* series is especially for kids who like numbers, doing puzzles, building with Legos™, and solving mysteries. These are all clues that you have an aptitude for math.

Read on to find some amazing ways to make math an important part of your future...

Surf the 'Net!

Type the words in **bold** in the Surf the 'Net sections into your favorite Internet search engine (like Google, Bing, or Yahoo) to find more information about the subject. Be sure to have permission and SUPERVISION from a trusted adult (like a teacher or parent) when going online.

Explore Some More!

In this book you'll find ideas you can use to explore cool resources in websites, in the news, and even in fun online games. Here's your chance to goof around and learn some more.

Ask Big Questions!

Curiosity opens the door to learning (and fun!). Ponder the questions posed here. Each question comes with an activity you can do. Use them to share your answers with others through posters, games, presentations, or even a good discussion where you consider both sides of an idea.

**Go online to download free activity sheets at
www.cherrylakepublishing.com/activities.**

Accountant

Surf the 'Net!

Explore how **money** works around the world.

What's your favorite thing? Do you love animals? Do you collect action figures? Do you enjoy playing and watching ice hockey? You can turn any interest into a career. All you have to do is become an **accountant**.

If you like animals, you can be an accountant for a zoo or a veterinarian. If you collect action figures, you can be an accountant for a toy company. Even pro-hockey teams need accountants. In fact, every business of every size needs someone to keep track of the money—as it comes in and as it goes out.

Accountants create financial records of money spent, saved, and received. Think about being an accountant for a zoo. The zoo sells tickets and season passes. The zoo sells plush toys and key chains in its gift shops. People donate money to the zoo. The city might also give money to the zoo. An accountant has to keep track of all these transactions.

But the zoo doesn't just earn money. The zoo spends money too. The accountant also has to count money going out to pay bills.

Where does the money go? Well, the elephants eat it. Just kidding. But they do eat lots of food. The zoo has to buy food for elephants and all the other animals. And don't forget food for human visitors!

The zoo has to pay for vet care and medicine. The zoo also has to make sure facilities are in good shape, both for animals and humans (think restrooms, animal habitats, and play areas).

Ask Big Questions!

Congratulations! You just hit the jackpot and won $1,000,000. So the big question is, **how are you going to spend all that money?** Set up a ledger and see how far the money goes. Be generous! Have fun! And don't forget to pay your taxes.

Explore Some More!

Find tips for managing your money at www.pbskids.org/itsmylife/money/managing.

It is very costly to run a zoo. An accountant must keep track of the **cash flow**, as money comes in and goes out.

Accountants also make sure other financial records are accurate too. Employees submit expense reports and budgets. Companies send bills. Bookkeepers keep ledgers and bank receipts. Accountants put all this information in their reports to figure out the **bottom line**.

Keeping accurate records is not just a good idea—it is also the law. Businesses must pay taxes, and these records let businesses know how much they owe.

Cha-ching!

Even zoos need accountants to crunch their numbers.

Actuary

RISK AHEAD

Surf the 'Net!

Search **charts and graphs for kids** to get acquainted with some of the tools actuaries use in their work.

Do you know where Tornado Alley is? You do if you are an **actuary**. An actuary knows which places are most likely to have big tornadoes—plus fires, floods, earthquakes, and hurricanes. An actuary studies **risk.** "Risk" is the chance something bad or expensive might happen.

Many actuaries work for **insurance** companies. To understand what an actuary does, you need to know what an insurance company does. An insurance company covers people, property, and businesses against future risks. Customers pay insurance companies premiums. If nothing happens, the insurance company keeps the money. When **disaster** strikes, insurance companies come to the rescue!

Here's how it works. Imagine a huge tornado rips through a town, and tears apart homes. Clothes, furniture, and cars are destroyed. When bad things like this happen, people thank their lucky stars for insurance. Their insurance policies cover the costs for replacing damaged and destroyed property. People can replace possessions and get on with life again.

Hurricane Katrina was the most expensive event in the history of insurance, and it hit Louisiana and Mississippi really hard. The risk of **storm surge** was underestimated and caused much more damage than expected. Lives were lost and neighborhoods wiped out. Actuaries and insurers learned important lessons from this disaster. They also paid out more than $60 billion in insurance claims!

Ask Big Questions!

Why are people who smoke considered a higher risk for insurance companies? Be a low-risk kid! Make a poster showing at least five things you can do to stay healthy and safe.

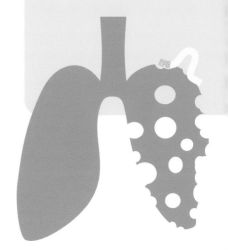

There are all kinds of risks besides natural disasters. Drive a motorcycle? That's a risk. Drive to work on a major highway? That's a risk. Work as a policeman? Fight fires? Don't exercise? Eat a poor diet? Smoke? Those are health risks. Actuaries study all these risks and tell insurance companies how much to charge people for insurance. The amount of money people pay is based on the risks people face.

Actuaries **analyze** the risks companies face too. They help businesses decide what kinds of insurance they need and how much coverage to buy. Being prepared makes a big difference when disaster strikes.

Explore Some More!

Speaking of natural disasters, learn more about them at **environment. nationalgeographic. com/environment/ natural-disasters/ forces-of-nature**.

Actuaries would call this a high-risk flood zone.

CAD Designer

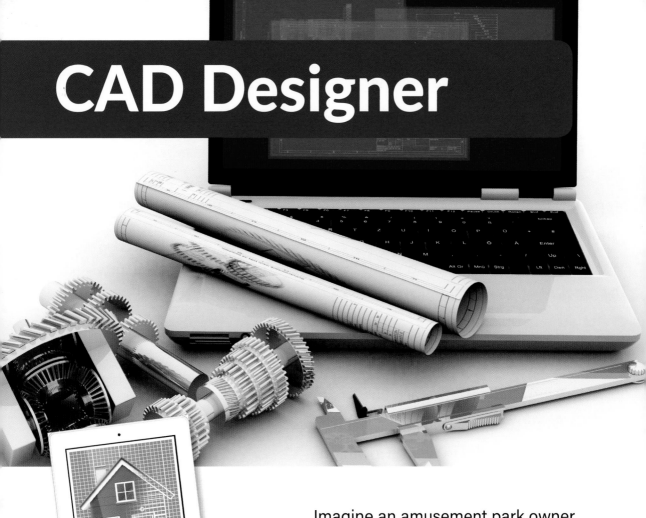

Surf the 'Net!

Search information about **drafting**, and then click on "images" to see some CAD drawings and tools.

Imagine an amusement park owner wants to add a new roller-coaster to the park. He wants one that has at least three hair-raising loops, and three gut-churning drops. The coaster must be three hundred feet away from the edge of the park. It must also be three hundred feet away from the nearest ride.

For something this dangerous, no one wants to rely on sloppy design. Someone has to make accurate measurements.

Someone has to take the designer's ideas and create drawings, or blueprints. Builders will rely on these to build a safe and awesome roller-coaster.

Perfect designs require precise planning. Precise plans rely on good math. This kind of precision requires computer-aided design, known as CAD for short.

CAD designers work closely with **engineers** to make important design decisions. Together they make careful calculations, using physics, the laws of gravity, and other safety rules. How high can the coaster be? How steep can the drops get? How fast can the ride go to provide a thrill without endangering its passengers? A CAD designer uses special computer technology to bring all these calculations together to create a very precise **blueprint** of the design.

Once the CAD files are perfected, builders use them to build the world's most amazing roller-coaster. Then it's time to buckle up and get ready to scream!

Ask Big Questions!

What would an ideal hangout for kids your age look like? Imagine that your parent agreed to let you design a room in your house. Use a ruler and graph paper to show your ideas. Be sure to include things like windows, doors, and snack bar!

Explore Some More!

Design your own thrilling roller coaster online at **www.discoverykids. com/games/build-a-coaster.**

Roller-coasters aren't the only things CAD designers work with. They draft plans for anything that must be built or manufactured. Houses, skyscrapers, ships, and automobiles are carefully planned with CAD. So are all the parts and pieces needed to build these things.

CAD designers also draft plans for land use. Highways, bridges, and even parking lots get their start in CAD. So do cartoons and special effects for movies.

CAD designers use numbers in creative ways. Their clever calculations turn ideas into reality.

All the fun started in a CAD plan!

Cryptologist

Do you ever do those fun code-breaker pages? You know, 1 = A, 2 = B, until you fill in the letters and find the secret message. You can do puzzles like these for a living—sort of!

Cryptography means "secret writing." Combine math with keeping secrets, and you have a mysterious job to do! If you like mysteries and puzzles, and are good at math, cryptology—making and breaking codes—might be your dream job.

Surf the Net!

Find out how **Navajo Code Talkers** made unbreakable codes to help the Allies of World War II.

Encrypted codes are used to protect and safely share secret information. **Cryptologists** work for government agencies, the military, computer companies, and banks.

People have been using cryptology to protect secrets and amuse themselves for thousands of years. The first known cryptography was **hieroglyphs** that early Egyptians carved into monuments.

Here's an example of how you use cryptology in everyday life. Say you go to the grocery store with your parents. After doing your best to sneak lots of goodies into the cart, you go to the checkout line. Your mom or dad moans and groans about how much everything costs. Then they swipe their credit or debit card to pay the bill. And there you have it—cryptology in action.

Huh?

Watch again. Your parent swipes a credit card and, thanks to the wonders of modern cryptology, your parents' information is safe. That's because the magnetic strip or

Ask Big Questions!

Can you make a code your friends and siblings can't crack? Give it a try by sending them a coded message using a secret code you create. For extra intrigue write out the code key in invisible ink!

chip in the credit card is embedded with vital information. Super secret codes verify your parent's identity and use cash in a bank account to actually pay the bill. Codes created by cryptologists keep this personal information private. Amazing, isn't it?

Keeping money safe is just one of the ways cryptology is used. Governments also use it to keep national secrets safe. The military uses cryptology to keep important communication private from enemies. Corporations use cryptology so spies cannot steal their ideas and inventions.

As hard as some cryptologists work to make secret codes, others work just as hard to crack them.

Explore Some More!

Crack the code at the Cybersecurity Awareness website at **www.nsa. gov/kids**.

What secrets do codes like these hold?

Economist

Surf the 'Net!

Learn more about what economists do by searching for economics for kids.

There's no such thing as a free lunch. It's one of the first rules of economics. Kids like you might disagree. You get all your lunches free, and breakfast and dinner too. But someone has to pay for them somewhere down the line. Cue a big "thank you" to parents everywhere!

Welcome to the world of **economists.** They look at how a nation's or business' wealth is created—and lost. To do this economists need to know a lot about how money and resources are used to produce and buy particular goods and services. It all comes down to the basic economic concept of supply and demand.

Supply is how many products or services are available. Demand is how much product and service consumers want to buy. In a healthy economy, demand for goods and services is high. Businesses flourish as they work to keep up with that demand. In a weak economy, demand is low, and businesses suffer.

Take a look at gas prices. Countries all over the world produce and sell fuel. When lots of customers want to buy lots of gasoline, demand is high, and so are prices. When there is more gasoline for sale than people want to buy, supply is high, and prices drop. Both situations can cause economic problems.

Economists look at factors like these to help governments, investors, and companies make smart decisions about money and resources. It boils down to

Ask Big Questions!

The stock market is an important part of a nation's economy. **What is the difference between a bull and bear market?** Make a poster to explain what this means in a way that kids like you can understand.

Explore Some More!

Bring home the bacon with fun and games at **www.bizkids.com/ games**.

how societies can use scarce resources to produce valuable **commodities** and distribute them among the world's people.

Economic advice and instructions are listened to by everyone, from presidents and world leaders, to individuals and corporations. Everyone benefits when the **economy** is strong and jobs are plentiful. People earn higher wages and can afford to pay for the things their families need or want.

Economics is about more than just money. Economics is also important to improve the living conditions of people everywhere.

Economists use charts and graphs to explain complicated financial information.

Sports Statistician

129 BALL ST -5.5
130 BUFFALO
162 MICHIGAN
163 UNLV
COL ST
N MEX ST
IDAHO
VIRGINIA
E CAROLNA
137 TEXAS A&M -1.5
138 KANSAS
139 S DIEGO S
140 BYU -27
141 RICE -2
142 TULANE
143 NAVY
144 AIR FORCE -3
145 STANFORD
146 NTRE DAME -32
147 W VIRGINI -26
148 MISS ST
149 LSU -2
150 FLORIDA
169 AKRON
170 CINCINATI
171 S CAR
172 KENTUCKY
173 BAYLOR
174 COLORADO
175 NEBRASKA
176 IOWA ST
177 MEMPHIS
178 ALA-BIRM
179 MISSOURI
180 TEX TECH
181 WEST MICH
182 OHIO
183 VANDY

Surf the 'Net!

For an intro to scorekeeping, search for **how to keep score in __________________.** Fill in the blank with the name of your favorite sport.

Do you have a favorite sport? Is it soccer? Football? Baseball? Golf? Sports are ultimately numbers games. Follow your favorite team or player, and you are bound to encounter lots of numbers—statistics, scores, rankings. It's all numbers, numbers, numbers!

Sports statisticians keep track of these numbers, recording **data** during games. They keep score, record times, and note exactly what plays each player makes during a game. When the game is over, statisticians enter the data into a computer. They are responsible for making official stats, so other people can learn from the data.

Thanks to technology, data has gotten even more important to sports. There was a time when scouts and coaches made decisions by watching players. Coaches now have access to all kinds of information about each player, like training, performance, and fitness level.

Many teams use sports statisticians as a secret weapon to help gain a competitive edge. These statisticians analyze data to help teams and players improve their skills and odds for winning. Here's how:

Let's say you coach a pro baseball team called the Hankies. You have to choose a starting pitcher for the next game against the Green Sox. You can use Leon Lefty or Reggie Righty. Your team's sports statistician says the Green Sox have nine batters. Six of them are left-handed. That's

Ask Big Questions!

How do statistics in sports work? Next time you watch a sports game on television, keep track of your favorite player's statistics. When the game is over, go online to the team's official website and see how closely your statistics match theirs.

a lot of lefties! Leon Lefty wins 35 percent more games than Reggie Righty against teams with more left-handed batters. Which pitcher should you choose?

The stats tell you to go with Leon for this game. He is more likely to win. Go Hankies!

Sports statisticians work with sports television networks. See the earpiece in the announcer's ear? A sports statistician is telling him interesting stats to share with the audience.

There's lots to be said for a job that combines math with sports. You get to follow your favorite teams. Plus, you always get the best seat in the house!

Explore Some More!

Check out the latest sports news at *Sports Illustrated Kids* at **www. sikids.com**.

Statistics play a big role in the game of golf.

Surveyor

Surf the 'Net!

Search for **famous land surveyors in history**. You are sure to discover some former U.S. presidents who were once surveyors.

Guess what? Your dad just earned a big bonus at work. The family gets to decide how to spend it. The choices are big—a ski trip or a swimming pool. Tough choices, but the family votes for—drumroll, please—a swimming pool!

Your family picks out the perfect pool, one with a slide and a hot tub. Then your dad gets all the permits needed to build a pool in your backyard. Before the digging starts, the city sends a **surveyor** to mark the boundaries between your property and the one next door. After all, you don't want to accidentally put half your hot tub in the neighbor's yard!

You've probably seen **surveyors** at work. They usually wear orange vests and look like they are taking pictures on the side of the road. What they are really doing is making precise measurements to determine property boundaries, or to map out the terrain of a specific area. The information is useful to engineers and mapmakers, and for construction and real estate purposes.

Surveyors also research the land they measure, asking lots of related questions. How many owners have there been over the years? When was the most recent survey? Do old measurements match?

Surveyors use tools such as raised tripods, distance measuring wheels, and survey markers (like flags). They draw boundary lines showing where the pool can—and can't—go.

Ask Big Questions!

In what ways has surveying changed over time? Find out what kinds of tools surveyors like George Washington and Abraham Lincoln used. Make a chart comparing the tools they used with the tools surveyors use today.

Explore Some More!

Practice your shape surveying skills at **www.funbrain.com/poly**.

Many of the tools surveyors now use are high tech. **Global positioning systems (GPS)** give them measurements from satellites orbiting in outer space! They can also make 3-D models of the land being surveyed with laser scanners. There are even remote control robots that help get even more precise measurements.

There is an old saying: "Measure twice; cut once." It means you should make sure your measurements are right before doing anything you cannot easily undo, such as putting in an in-ground swimming pool. That way surveyors help property owners stay friendly with their neighbors.

Surveyors use high-tech tools to make accurate measurements.

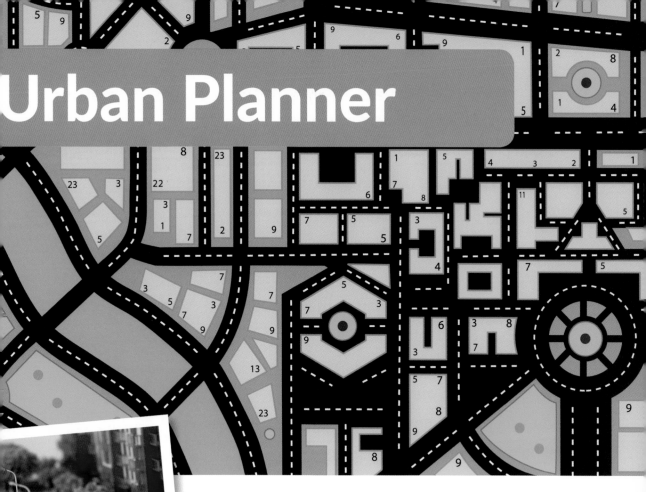

Urban Planner

In every city or town, there is private property where people live and run businesses. There is also public property people share, like schools, churches, parks, and playgrounds. Open space is another important part of a well-planned city. Striking the right mix of private, public, and open property is what **urban planners** get paid to do.

Pretend the city council has decided the city needs a new playground. But it's a big

Surf the Net!

Find examples of **best urban planning** and **livable cities**.

city, and someone needs to figure out the best place to put one. It's time to bring in an urban planner.

An urban planner looks at where people are located. Maybe new neighborhoods are growing quickly in one part of the town, so the kids there need more space to play. Or perhaps a big apartment complex is planned on the other side of town, so the children who will live there need a playground, and maybe a recreation center too. An urban planner gathers information about all the options to help city leaders decide the best place to put the new family-friendly facilities.

The growing area might also need a school, offices, shops, roads, parks, and all the other things people like to have nearby. Urban planners help decide where all these will be built. Most of all, the job of an urban planner is about making cities good places to live, work, and play.

Sometimes urban planners get to start from scratch and design brand new communities. Sometimes they help imagine

Ask Big Questions!

If you were an urban planner, what three things would you change about your own neighborhood? Make a before and after poster using images you find online and photos of your neighborhood.

brand new cities too. This happened in Kapolei, Hawaii. What was once sugarcane and pineapple fields is now home to more than 100,000 people. Kapolei is a master-planned community and known locally as the "second city" of Oahu.

Urban planners need sharp math skills, but they also need good people skills. They work hard to keep everyone happy with what is being built. They can't think only about what makes sense now. They have to think about the future too, by designing cities people can enjoy for many generations to come.

Explore Some More!

Build your own online city at www. planitgreenlive.com/en/ build-your-own-city.

Designing spaces where people live, work, and play is what urban planners do.

Find *Your* Future in Mathematics

Let's review the amazing career ideas you've just discovered. Below are descriptions of some of the opportunities waiting for people who like math. Read them and see if you can match them with the correct job titles.

Instead of writing in this book, use a separate sheet of paper to write your answers. Even better, download a free activity sheet at www.cherrylakepublishing.com/activities.

A Accountant

B Actuary

C CAD designer

D Cryptologist

E Economist

F Sports statistician

G Surveyor

H Urban planner

1 Designing and planning communities and forecasting the future needs of cities

2 Estimating the risk and likely cost of major events, such as death, sickness, injury, disability, or loss of property

3 Keeping track of what businesses earn and spend

4 Measuring property boundaries

5 Creating and cracking codes

6 Creating very precise blueprints used in building and manufacturing

7 Recording every move an athlete or team makes during a game

8 Studying supply and demand of a resource or product

(Answer Key: 1-H; 2-B; 3-A; 4-G; 5-D; 6-C; 7-F; 8-E)

Glossary

accountant person who keeps the financial records of another person or business

actuary person who compiles and analyzes statistics and uses them to calculate insurance risks and premiums

analyze to investigate an item, theory, set of numbers, or data, and come to a conclusion

blueprint design plan or other technical drawing

bottom line the final total of an account, balance sheet, or other financial document

CAD designer person who uses special software to create precise drawings or technical illustrations used by architects, engineers, drafters, artists, and manufacturers

cash flow the amount of money going in and out of a business

commodity raw material or agricultural product that can be bought and sold, such as copper or coffee

cryptologist person who uses mathematics, such as number theory, and applies formulas and algorithms to create and decipher codes

data set of facts

disaster sudden cause of loss, suffering, or damage

economy the wealth and resources of a country or region

economist person who studies the flow of cash and credit between people, institutions, and banks, and studies the health of the economy and ways to improve living conditions

engineer scientist who builds things

global positioning system (GPS) satellite-powered navigation system that allows people to determine their exact locations at any given time and in all weather conditions

hieroglyphs picture of an object representing a word, syllable, or sound, as found in ancient Egyptian and other writing systems

insurance payment to a company that agrees to pay back money in the event of unfortunate circumstances or accidents

risk chance of damage, injury, liability, or loss

sports statistician person who collects and studies data related to a specific sport, sports team, or individual players

storm surge abnormal rise in the level of seawater generated by a storm

surveyor person who determines the size, shape, or boundaries of pieces of land

urban planner person who deals with the design and organization of urban space and activities in cities and urban spaces

Index

About the Author

Kelly Gunzenhauser is the author or co-author of several books for teachers and students, including *The Big Honkin' Activity Book* (published by Lark Books). Her interest in helping kids choose careers is particularly strong right now, since her two boys, Casey and Reid, will be doing just that in a few years. Kelly lives in Winston-Salem, North Carolina, with her boys, her husband Eric, and Bandit, the pizza-stealing beagle.